TRACKSIDE
around the TWIN CITIES
with JOE ELLIOTT
1968-1972

by Aaron Isaacs

Copyright © 2008
Morning Sun Books, Inc.

All rights reserved. This book may not be reproduced in part or in whole without written permission from the publisher, except in the case of brief quotations or reproductions of the cover for the purposes of review.

Library of Congress
Catalog Card No. 2008924105

First Printing
ISBN 1-58248-244-6

Published by
Morning Sun Books, Inc.
9 Pheasant Lane
Scotch Plains, NJ 07076
Printed in Korea

Robert J. Yanosey, President
To access our full library *In Color* visit us at
www.morningsunbooks.com

Acknowledgements

Joe Elliott was not a passive partner in this work. He helped me with his biography, supplied additional photos and participated actively in the production stage of the book, since he lives close to the publisher. He helped identify the locations of some of the photos. For the most part, they were not captioned when I received them, so it has been a challenge to recall what we are seeing. My good friend John Diers also helped identify a number of photo locations and passenger trains (is that the BADGER or the DAKOTAN?). Hopefully they're all correct, and I apologize for any inaccuracies.

After Joe moved on from railfan photography to his adult life's work in industrial archeology, he gave away his slides. Roughly half went to the author, and the other half to John Cartwright, a Twin Cities railfan and pen and ink artist who specializes in drawing the depots of Minnesota and surrounding states. His pen and ink drawings of the St. Paul Union Depot and the Minneapolis Great Northern and Milwaukee Road depots introduce those sections of the book. John loaned me his Elliott slides and I mixed them up so thoroughly I no longer know whose are whose. John graciously consented to let me use them for the book with this blanket credit.

Finally, my thanks to Bob Yanosey and Morning Sun Books for making this volume possible. I've wanted to do it for 30 years, and when I suggested it to Bob, he quickly gave his approval. Although there is a uniform book size, Morning Sun lets its authors fill the 128 pages as they see fit with minimal oversight, and for that I am grateful.

Table of Contents

Trackside Photographer, Joe Elliott 3	St. Anthony Tower 63-71
Author, Aaron Isaacs 3	Dinkytown 72-74
Twin Cities Railroading 4-5	Stone Arch Bridge 75-79
St. Paul Union Depot .6-22	Great Northern depot .80-92
Dayton's Bluff 23-27	Great Northern Willmar Line, Monticello Line . . .93-97
Newport and points south 28-30	Great Northern Depot to Coon Creek Junction . . .98-107
Milwaukee Road Short Line to Minneapolis 31-35	Soo Line, west to east 108-115
South Minneapolis engine terminal 36-38	Minneapolis Northfield & Southern 116-118
Milwaukee Depot 39-46	Other and outstate 119
Milwaukee Road to Hopkins 47-48	Hudson 120-123
SPUD to Westminster Junction and Trout Brook Jct. .49-59	Hinkley Tower 124-127
Great Northern mainline to Minneapolis 60-62	Joe goes black and white 128

A Word About Photo Dates

While the author is confident that the photos in this book were taken during the period 1968-72, most of them were not dated when they were taken. However, two important events had a major impact on the trains Joe was photographing. The Burlington Northern merger of the Great Northern, Northern Pacific and Chicago, Burlington & Quincy occurred in 1970. Amtrak's takeover of the national passenger train system happened in 1971.

TRACKSIDE around the TWIN CITIES with JOE ELLIOTT 1968-1972

Trackside Photographer, Joe Elliott

I met Joe Elliott when we both attended the University of Minnesota in 1970. By then he had been shooting color slides around the Twin Cities for several years. He started in 35mm, but soon purchased a twin lens reflex camera, which produced oversized slides 2 1/4 inches square.

Joe had (and still has) a terrific photographer's eye. By the time I met him, he had begun to move from simple documentation toward art, using angles of view, lighting and often a telephoto lens to enhance every scene. He was also moving into black and white photography, which would become his preferred medium.

I accompanied him on a number of photo trips around the Twin Cities. He was always extremely careful selecting and composing his shots. I remember wondering how someone could take so much time setting up for a shot, but he would not be hurried. After seeing his work, I actually stopped taking train photos for about 15 years, because I knew I would never be in his league.

After college, Joe spent a year as a working railroader. He hired out as a brakeman with the Chicago & North Western, working various yards around town and runs to Altoona, Wisconsin, Albert Lea, Minnesota, and Oelwein, Iowa. In 1975, Joe and his wife Betsy moved to Brooklyn, New York to pursue graduate degrees, in fine arts at Pratt Institute, and in education at Bank Street College of Education. Making a living in the arts is never easy, and for years Joe's primary source of income was carpentry.

Photographically, Joe had moved almost exclusively into black and white, using a 4 X 5 view camera. Although he still occasionally shot trains, his preferred subject was industrial archaeology. Heavy industry was deserting the northeast, leaving behind the hulks of abandoned factories, empty mines, waterfront piers, rail yards, and forgotten working class towns. Joe found himself attracted to them, catching them in the half-life between operation and demolition. He began to produce exquisite portraits of rust and decay, informed by the work of famous photographers such as David Plowden, Walker Evans, and Charles Sheeler. Joe began to get contract work recording endangered facilities for the Historic American Engineering Record (HAER), an ongoing project of the Department of the Interior to record historic structures before they were lost. He became active in the Society for Industrial Archaeology.

Joe Elliott in 1990

In 1983, Joe was finally able to work full time in his chosen field, as a professor of Art at Muhlenberg College in Allentown, a small industrial city in eastern Pennsylvania. He has been there ever since, teaching and continuing to work for HAER. Perhaps his most spectacular recent effort was documenting the Bethlehem Steel works in its last years of operation. A book on that project is in process.

In preparing this book, I asked Joe if he was aware that he was documenting the end of an era. Yes, he replied. He knew the death of the privately operated passenger train was imminent, that smaller railroads were losing their identities through mergers and that technology endangered the station agents and tower operators. He says he felt a sense of urgency, trying to record these things before it was too late. It was the beginning of a career doing just that, documenting the receding industrial environment for future generations.

Author, Aaron Isaacs

Aaron Isaacs has been a lifelong railfan, inheriting the interest from his father, George Isaacs. A Twin Cities resident since 1958, he has been active in rail preservation for over 30 years. He's a past president of the Minnesota Transportation Museum, and edited that organization's *Minnegazette* magazine from 1990 to 2007. He now edits the *Twin City Lines* magazine for the Minnesota Streetcar Museum, serves on the MSM board and keeps their photo archive. Since 1996 he has also edited *Railway Museum Quarterly* for the Association of Railway Museums. In 2007, he co-authored with John Diers the book *Twin Cities by Trolley* for the University of Minnesota Press.

Aaron Isaacs

Twin Cities Railroading

In terms of railroad infrastructure and railfan appeal, the Twin Cities have always been a two-for-one bonanza.

Most large cities feature a web of interconnecting railroads centered on a single downtown. In Minneapolis-St. Paul there are two downtowns, so everything happened twice. Located ten miles apart, each downtown had major passenger stations. With only a couple of exceptions, each railroad maintained yards, engine facilities and freight houses in both cities. In 1945, the Twin Cities still sported 20 roundhouses. Even in 1970, at least eight of them were still in use.

The Twin Cities were served by nine Class 1 lines, including Great Northern, Northern Pacific, Burlington, Rock Island, Milwaukee Road, Chicago & North Western, Chicago Great Western, Soo Line and Minneapolis & St. Louis. Add to this the subsidiary carriers Chicago, St. Paul, Minneapolis & Omaha and Wisconsin Central, plus local short lines Minneapolis Northfield & Southern, and Minneapolis, Anoka & Cuyuna Range, plus switching road Minnesota Transfer and St. Paul Union Depot Company, and there was plenty of variety.

More than just a big rail center, the Twin Cities was a railroad headquarters town. Great Northern and Northern Pacific occupied matching adjacent office buildings in downtown St. Paul that appeared to be a single structure but were connected on only one floor. Despite being operated as part of the C&NW, the Omaha Road still maintained its general offices in St. Paul. Minneapolis hosted the headquarters buildings of the Soo Line and the Minneapolis & St. Louis, plus the local short lines.

By the time Joe photographed these railroads, the merger movement was well underway. M&StL, Minnesota Western, Minneapolis Eastern and CGW had been absorbed into C&NW, although paint schemes and operations still revealed their old corporate roots. In 1970, GN, NP and CB&Q merged into the Burlington Northern, but there was plenty of heritage painted equipment still on the loose. Elsewhere, Soo Line was still independent, along with the Minneapolis, Northfield & Southern, known locally as the "Dan Patch." The Milwaukee Road and Rock Island were sliding toward bankruptcy, but were still running by themselves. The Minnesota Transfer, owned in common by the Class Ones but locally managed, still deployed its olive green switchers.

Joe captured the end of the pre-Amtrak passenger trains. The Chicago Great Western and Soo Line had gone freight-only shortly before he began shooting, and the Rock Island quit its last passenger train shortly thereafter. However, the MORNING and AFTERNOON ZEPHYRS, BLACK HAWK, NORTH COAST LIMITED, MAINSTREETER, EMPIRE BUILDER, WESTERN STAR, GOPHER and BADGER , WINNIPEG LIMITED, DAKOTAN, MORNING and AFTERNOON HIAWATHAS, PIONEER LIMITED and FAST MAIL still passed through, in high style until almost the end.

Much has changed since Joe took the last of these slides in 1972. Passenger service is now limited to the once daily Amtrak EMPIRE

BUILDER. Minneapolis' Great Northern depot is gone and its Milwaukee Road depot, while intact with its train shed, is now a landlocked hotel. The St. Paul Union Depot, shorn of trains, is scheduled to resume that role in ten years or so, replacing the Amtrak station located in the former Minnesota Transfer Midway yards.

Mergers have reduced the local class ones to three, BNSF, Canadian Pacific and Union Pacific. With the exception of the Soo Line Building in Minneapolis, the corporate headquarters are gone. Most of the large local shop complexes have also disappeared, including Soo Line's Shoreham Shops, GN's Dale Street locomotive shops, Jackson Street car shop, Mississippi Street coach shop and Minneapolis Junction roundhouse, NP's Como car shops, the St. Paul coach yard with its commissary and Mississippi Street roundhouse, M&StL's Cedar Lake Shops, C&NW's East Minneapolis and East St. Paul roundhouses, the St. Paul Union Depot's roundhouse and the Dan Patch's Glenwood engine house. Almost all the freight houses are gone, except for a couple that sur-

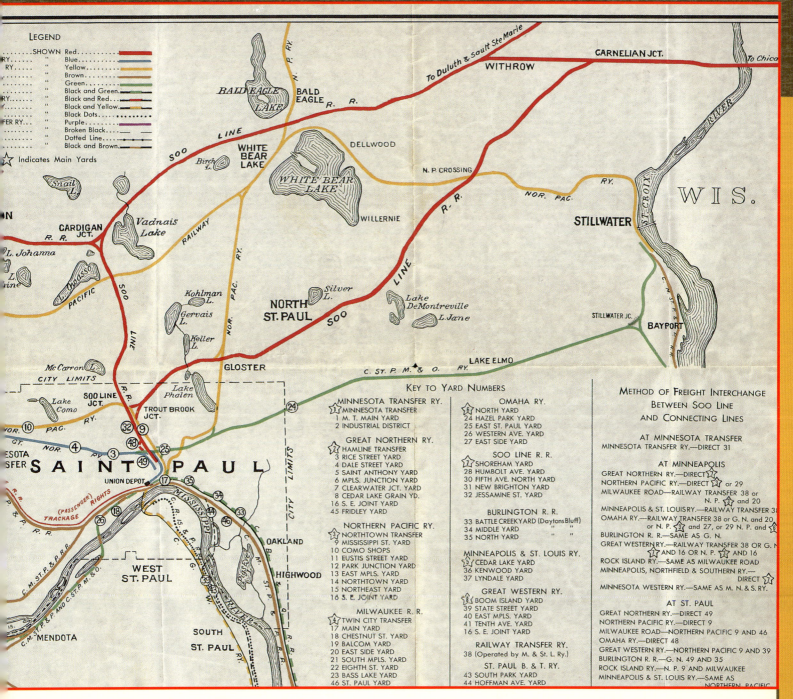

vive as condos and industrial buildings. Gone too are the manned towers and cabooses.

Quite a bit of track has disappeared, including all the rail yards and industrial tracks adjacent to downtown Minneapolis. The rails are gone from the Stone Arch Bridge across St. Anthony Falls. One can now ride a bicycle on miles of former right of way, and the Hiawatha light rail line has replaced the Milwaukee Road leading southeast from downtown Minneapolis. The good news is that most of the old hot spots for train watching are now hotter than ever as traffic has increased.

Even today, the Twin Cities are not a featureless sea of wide cabs. The Minnesota Transfer is now the independently owned Minnesota Commercial, known for its eclectic roster of vintage diesels. Besides working the historic MT trackage, it has taken over a number of local switching and branch lines from the class ones. It is headquartered at the last fully operational roundhouse in town. Built to house only switch engines, it has an unusually short turntable and was constructed in several architecturally distinct segments over the period 1891-1950.

The regional Twin Cities & Western has taken over the old Milwaukee Road mainline to the South Dakota boarder, plus the surviving portion of the M&StL's Watertown, SD line. Short line Progressive Rail is running portions of the old Minneapolis, Northfield & Southern and has revived that road's vintage color scheme and even some of its motive power. In 2009, Northstar commuter train service will begin between Minneapolis and Big Lake.

Looking back, it's clear that Joe Elliott captured the end of two eras, the privately operated passenger train and pre-merger class one railroading. He also caught the last years of manned depots and towers and wood cabooses. The large majority of Joe's photos have never been published. We hope you enjoy them.

St. Paul Union Depot

Here are two big cities with downtowns only ten miles apart, but that was no reason not to have big passenger stations in both cities. Minneapolis may have been the bigger and more dynamic of the twins, but its trains were divided between two depots, while St. Paul sported a true Union Depot. It served all the trains of all the railroads—no exceptions. The original union depot was built in 1881. A Victorian pile with a large train shed, it burned for the second time in 1913. The fire created an excuse to build a modern, much larger facility to replace its cramped forebear. The St. Paul Union Depot Company, (unfortunately its initials spelled SPUD) built the new depot directly north of the old one and elevated the tracks above the level of periodic Mississippi River flooding. Passenger traffic was already in decline when the new SPUD opened in stages from 1920 to 1926, but it was a magnificent facility.

SPUD was a run-through station for the Milwaukee Road, Rock Island, Soo Line and Chicago Great Western. It was a stub operation for everyone else. They had two choices—back in or out using the east wye, or run the power around the train. The CB&Q, GN and NP did the former, the C&NW the latter, dragging its consists backwards between Minneapolis and St. Paul. Except for the NP's Duluth trains, all NP and GN trains terminated in St. Paul or swapped for CB&Q power if they continued to Chicago, so the stub arrangement was less problematic.

SPUD was shut down immediately on Amtrak day, and was eventually replaced by a new structure located in the Midway (halfway between the downtowns) on the site of a former Minnesota Transfer yard. The depot head house has since been revived with restaurant and office tenants. Meanwhile, the concourse over the tracks, as well as the land under it, were purchased by the adjacent Post Office. The concourse has sat vacant and deteriorating since the early 1970s.

Things are about to change for the better. The City of St. Paul and Ramsey County are determined to return trains to the depot, and upgrade it into a multi-modal transportation center. With assistance from powerful Minnesota Congressman James Oberstar, they are close to an agreement to purchase the land and concourse from the Post Office. The plan is to bring back Amtrak, institute commuter rail to Minneapolis and Hastings, and terminate both buses and the Central Corridor light rail line there. Hopefully in the future it will host high-speed rail to Chicago.

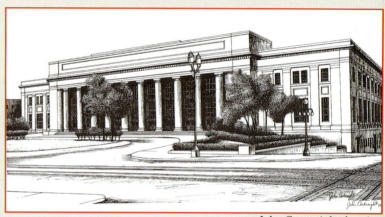

John Cartwright drawing

ABOVE ■ The St. Paul Union Depot Company, which was run by the Minnesota Transfer, owned a single GE 44-ton center cab. Some railroads, notably Great Northern, did their own switching at SPUD.

LEFT ■ Headlight extinguished, the North Coast is backing into the St. Paul Union Depot. There it will be combined with the EMPIRE BUILDER and MORNING ZEPHYR, and receive new power for the trip to Chicago.

BELOW ■ Even though it's now all Burlington Northern, the NORTH COAST LIMITED continues to change power at St. Paul Union Depot. The former Northern Pacific F-units are cut off and replaced by CB&Q E-units (this one in BN paint).

BELOW ■ Its duty over for today, this NORTH COAST LIMITED F-unit set picks its way through the double-slip switches on its way the former NP Mississippi Street roundhouse for servicing. Because of the BN merger, that facility would soon be surplus. St. Paul engine servicing was consolidated at the modest CB&Q Dayton's Bluff facility one mile to the right. Note the passenger cars in the NP coach yard in the distance.

ABOVE ■ Behind E7 #512, which still has its mars light, the DAKOTAN to Fargo backs into the depot to prepare for departure. Note the yellow track number signs at the ends of the umbrella sheds.

OPPOSITE PAGE, TOP ■ After closing its Jackson Street roundhouse in 1959, GN based its passenger power at the Union Depot roundhouse. It was located in the center of the wye at the east end of the depot throat. The curving tracks at right lead into the depot. The tracks in the foreground bypass the depot and connect the throat of tracks past Dayton's Bluff (to the left out of the frame) with the equally busy tracks up the valley of Trout Brook (to the right). Note the steam generator/power car, built from an old B unit. This view looks down from the 3rd Street viaduct.

RIGHT ■ The WESTERN STAR, with a new SDP40 trailing, passes the SPUD east tower. The First National Bank building, tallest in downtown St. Paul, towers at right. Directly behind the diesels is the St. Paul Downtown Post Office. Like most such facilities, it was located directly adjacent to the Union Depot.

ABOVE & BELOW ■ Former Great Northern passenger power receives attention at the St. Paul Union Depot roundhouse. The 500-class E7s were purchased for the 1947 EMPIRE BUILDER but couldn't handle the mountain grades. They spent the rest of their careers on short distance trains within Minnesota and North Dakota, the GOPHER and BADGER to Duluth, the RED RIVER and DAKOTAN, plus the WINNIPEG LIMITED. The F-units handled the EMPIRE BUILDER and the WESTERN STAR.

ABOVE ■ The late evening summer sun illuminates the AFTERNOON HIAWATHA as it enters SPUD from Chicago. This train was eliminated in 1970, and the MORNING HIAWATHA lost its Skytop observation at the same time.

BELOW ■ The MORNING HIAWATHA receives baggage at St. Paul.

The westbound MORNING HIAWATHA enters the east end of the depot throat, passing the CB&Q Division Street tower at left. The Milwaukee Road freight tracks that bypass the depot are atop the wall at right.

The AFTERNOON HIAWATHA curves out of SPUD.

RIGHT ■ The MORNING HIAWATHA was scheduled to leave St. Paul for Chicago at 8:05 AM, followed five minutes later by the combined MORNING ZEPHYR/EMPIRE BUILDER/NORTH COAST LIMITED. They raced down the Mississippi and crossed each other's path three minutes apart at La Crosse, 129 miles away. Despite its later departure, the Q delivered its monster train to Chicago Union Station at 2:55 PM, 15 minutes earlier and 20 minutes faster overall than the Milwaukee. The Milwaukee made it to Chicago in seven hours and 15 minutes. Compensating for the difference in St. Paul depot locations, Amtrak takes eight hours and five minutes to cover the same route today.

ABOVE ■ The AFTERNOON HIAWATHA prepares to leave St. Paul for Chicago. Note the Alco switcher on loan from SPUD parent Minnesota Transfer.

Train 57, the FAST MAIL, has arrived at St. Paul. It carried no passengers, although its eastbound counterpart, Train 56 did. This view looks west from the depot at the Robert Street and Wabasha Street bridges over the Mississippi.

BELOW ■ Train 56, the FAST MAIL to Chicago, leaves SPUD. Unlike its westbound counterpart, this train carried passengers, albeit in a single rider coach. Its 8:15 PM departure from St. Paul made it convenient for evening passengers bound for Winona and La Crosse, both large college towns. The Milwaukee Road always carried the bulk of the Chicago–Twin Cities mail, and this train was assigned two full-length RPO cars.

ABOVE ■ The overnight BLACK HAWK from Chicago meets the eastbound NORTH COAST LIMITED, trailing a business car. The trains are under the west end of the depot concourse.

LEFT ■ The MORNING ZEPHYR has arrived from Chicago and is off-loading baggage. This view looks out the west end of the depot. It will return a couple of hours later as the AFTERNOON ZEPHYR. They share the same abbreviated consist, unlike their opposite numbers, which were combined with the EMPIRE BUILDER and NORTH COAST LIMITED.

ABOVE ■ A proper Minnesota winter looks like this. The temperature is well below zero, which causes everything to steam. Some of that steam appears to have condensed on the air horn of the MORNING ZEPHYR'S E-unit. A crew member has climbed up there with a fusee to thaw it out.

RIGHT ■ On a subzero winter day, ice clings to the baggage car trucks of a Duluth train as it backs into the depot. The addition of an SDP40 to the usual E7 may be because of a longer than normal consist, or more likely to add steam generator capacity to keep the train from freezing up.

ABOVE ■ Freight tracks bypassed the train sheds of St. Paul Union Depot. They belonged to the Milwaukee Road. The C&NW and Chicago Great Western also had trackage rights. This C&NW freight is probably a transfer from the Western Avenue Yard, a mile west of SPUD along the Mississippi River, to the former CGW Hoffman Avenue Yard near Dayton's Bluff.

BELOW ■ In the 1960s the Soo Line secured trackage rights over the Chicago Great Western to serve the large refinery at Pine Bend, MN, about ten miles south of St. Paul. For the first time, this brought Soo freight past SPUD. This train is taking the northwest leg of the wye just east of SPUD. It will follow the former Northern Pacific to Trout Brook Junction, there reaching its own St. Paul branch to Cardigan Junction, and from there will head west to Shoreham Yard.

ABOVE ■ The Milwaukee Road's Twin Cities transfer runs were a banquet of old and/or minority diesels. This book has no photos of them, but Fairbanks Morse baby Train Masters drilled the downtown St. Paul intermodal yard. The transfers featured F-units, aging six-axle Alcos, and my favorite, a handful of Baldwin AS616s. Given the challenging Short Line hill, their "chuggin' and luggin'" characteristics were put to good use. This set is passing the St. Paul Union Depot.

RIGHT ■ There is no question of who owned this coach yard and commissary. The Northern Pacific was proud of its trains and marketed them. All through the 1970s, the "The Vista Dome NORTH COAST LIMITED" was advertised frequently on TV, radio and in the newspapers. The company's motto, "Main Street of the Northwest" appeared on locomotives, freight cars and cabooses, and inspired the train name MAINSTREETER.

18

ABOVE ■ The Northern Pacific coach yard and commissary was located just east of the St. Paul Union Depot. Home of the legendary "Big Baked Potato", the commissary's activities are well chronicled in the book "Dining Car Line to the Pacific."

BELOW ■ An ore train rolls under 3rd Street and passes the SPUD roundhouse. The official riding the rear end may be inspecting the ex-NP Skally Line as part of the merger's track consolidation program. Having inherited two parallel railroads between the Twin Cities and Duluth, BN decided the former NP was surplus and abandoned most it. This portion is now a trail.

RIGHT ■ Brake shoes smoking behind Big Sky Blue Fs, a solid iron ore extra reaches the bottom of the steep, twisting former NP "Skally" Line that reached SPUD via the valley of Phalen Creek, just north of the NP commissary. Most ore moves in trains to Lake Superior, where it is transferred to lake boats for the run to Chicago, Detroit, Cleveland or other Lake Erie ports. This is probably the all-rail move to the steel mill in Granite City, IL.

Dayton's Bluff

The railroads that follow the east bank of the Mississippi must squeeze past Dayton's Bluff to reach downtown St. Paul. The CB&Q and the Milwaukee Road paired their lines through here to create a double-track railroad. The Rock Island used it north from Newport Tower via trackage rights. A later addition was the Chicago Great Western's trains via subsidiary St. Paul Bridge and Terminal, absorbed by 1968 into the C&NW. Not only was there a great deal of traffic (there's even more today), Dayton's Bluff was where trains sorted out their diverging routes to the north or south, so there was plenty of crossing between tracks.

LEFT & RIGHT ■ When the monstrous combined MORNING ZEPHYR/EMPIRE BUILDER/NORTH COAST LIMITED accelerated away from St. Paul, its four E-units had to burn off some accumulated carbon, blanketing Dayton's Bluff in a daily exhaust cloud that would bring down the regulators today. The Milwaukee Road's first intermodal yard occupies the Old Yard that hugs the river at right.

BELOW ■ The last gasp of Rock Island's passenger service to the Twin Cities, now named the PLAINSMAN, arrives in St. Paul after a daytime run from Kansas City. Until the mid-60s, the Rock ran twice daily to Kansas City and the TWIN STAR ROCKET made the longest north-south run in the United States, 1368 miles from Minneapolis to Houston. In addition, the ZEPHYR-ROCKET, jointly operated with the Burlington, passed through here on the way to St. Louis.

Above ■ A BN SD9 passes Division Street Tower in the company of Rock Island and Milwaukee Road freights, just east of St. Paul Union Depot. Note the weeds, lack of ballast, low joints and hand-throw switches, all because this was historically where the Burlington ended and the GN and NP began. This track was the home of lowly transfer drags between the independent carriers' yards. Today these same tracks see dozens of transcontinental through freights daily. They have been upgraded with heavy welded rail, sitting on high ballast. The tower is long gone and CTC-controlled power switches speed the crossovers at Dayton's Bluff. As this is written, however, some of the SD9s are still active around town on the BN, so some things haven't changed.

It gets very busy just east of the St. Paul Union Depot, where the tracks funnel past Dayton's Bluff. The Milwaukee Road Baldwin is switching the Old Yard, originally used for l.c.l. and express, and converted into an early intermodal facility. It has since been replaced by a newer Canadian Pacific facility next to Shoreham Yard in northeast Minneapolis. A C&NW local from the Western Avenue Yard will soon enter the former CGW St. Paul Bridge & Terminal trackage to switch riverfront grain terminals. At right, a BN through freight heads up the hill toward Westminster Junction and Minneapolis.

LEFT ■ A Milwaukee Road mixed freight and Burlington Northern ore train wait at Dayton's Bluff to see who will get the high green. The ore train has lower a speed limit, so by all rights the Milwaukee should be given a head start.

BELOW ■ The MORNING HIAWATHA threads its way through typical traffic at the Dayton's Bluff bottleneck. The freight at left could be headed either to the Milwaukee's South Minneapolis Yard, or to the Ford Plant. Note the track scale at right.

25

LEFT ■ Viewed from the Warner Road overpass, the combined EMPIRE BUILDER/NORTH COAST LIMITED accelerates past Dayton's Bluff as a steam generator pops off. There are no ex-CB&Q domes at the head of this consist, indicating that the MORNING ZEPHYR may be running separately today. The trains were more likely to be separated in the peak summer season. St. Paul Union Depot lies beyond the storage tank at upper left. The domed building at upper right is the Minnesota state capitol.

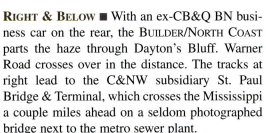

RIGHT & BELOW ■ With an ex-CB&Q BN business car on the rear, the BUILDER/NORTH COAST parts the haze through Dayton's Bluff. Warner Road crosses over in the distance. The tracks at right lead to the C&NW subsidiary St. Paul Bridge & Terminal, which crosses the Mississippi a couple miles ahead on a seldom photographed bridge next to the metro sewer plant.

Above ■ A South Minneapolis transfer climbs the freight bypass around the St. Paul Union Depot. The yard at right was originally used for l.c.l. and later a trailer ramp. It has been replaced by park land.

Right ■ The same train heads away from the camera. It's actually running on the original CB&Q rails. The Milwaukee Road, built earlier, is the other track. North Star Steel, the Twin Cities' only steel mill, is at right. It is switched by Canadian Pacific, which now owns the Milwaukee.

Below ■ Passing the south end of the Milwaukee Road Pig's Eye Yard, four Es elephant style propel the Builder/North Coast at high speed along Highway 61. Note the three silver Burlington coaches, including one high-roofed heavyweight, behind the first baggage car. That's all that's left of the Morning Zephyr.

Newport Tower and points south

The Milwaukee Road in 1869 and the Burlington in 1887 built parallel single track railroads up the Mississippi from St. Croix Tower (across the river from Hastings) to SPUD. In 1892 they entered into a mutual trackage rights agreement to operate their lines as a double track railroad. In 1901, the Rock Island opened its bridge across the Mississippi from Inver Grove. It negotiated rights to use the joint Q-Milwaukee line and entered it at Newport Tower. The tower also sorted out who would use which line to the south. The Burlington's route was more circuitous so it descended to the river on a gentler grade. After its retirement, the tower was purchased by the Newport Model Railroad Club, moved a short distance away and restored.

ABOVE ■ An all-CB&Q lashup passes Newport Tower. Besides meeting the Rock Island, the Milwaukee Road and CB&Q mainlines crossed here.

RIGHT ■ The Burlington and Milwaukee Road lines between St. Paul and St. Croix Tower had to descend the Mississippi River bluffs and did so on completely different alignments down parallel ravines. The Milwaukee's line was shorter and steeper, and the combined BUILDER/NORTH COAST is descending it today toward the lower grade CB&Q alignment. Hastings is in the distance.

LEFT ■ Alco RSC3 #594 switched the mills at Red Wing, but its light axle loading was essential to its other duty, treading the Chicago Great Western's doubtful rail up the Cannon River valley to Cannon Falls. Until 1937, the Milwaukee had its own parallel line up the river, but since then had run on trackage rights to reach a stub of its own line in Cannon Falls. The Red Wing depot remains in service today as an Amtrak stop.

RIGHT ■ The Milwaukee Road follows the scenic west bank of the Mississippi for 110 miles from Hastings to LaCrosse. Arguably the most scenic stretch is along Lake Pepin, where the river is at its widest between Lake City and Wabasha. The numerous curves in this stretch limit speed to 70 miles per hour. In this sequence, the AFTERNOON HIAWATHA leans into one of the curves on a fill built into the river.

BELOW ■ Besides the HIAWATHA itself, this picture is full of past railroad practices that will never return, starting with the Railway Express boxcar. The jointed rail has been replaced with welded. The double track with automatic block signals is now single track with Centralized Traffic Control. The track speeder in the distance has been replaced by a hi-rail truck. Alongside is the last active telegraph line into the Twin Cities, which finally went dead around 1973.

ABOVE ■ Across the valley, the EMPIRE BUILDER sped up the Burlington as it followed the east bank of the Mississippi. Both lines were double tracked, and the BNSF remains so today, while the ex-Milwaukee Road has been single tracked. The CB&Q was better engineered than the Milwaukee and featured higher speeds.

Passing the smoke from a brush fire, a BN freight headed by an ex-GN F45 rolls south along the Wisconsin side of the Mississippi.

Milwaukee Road Short Line to Minneapolis

Headed up the Mississippi River from the St. Paul Union Depot, the Milwaukee Road and the Chicago & North Western shared track as far as Cliff Junction, about two miles from downtown. In 1880, the Milwaukee branched off this line at Chestnut Street on the west edge of downtown, and built its Short Line to Minneapolis, replacing the circuitous route via Mendota. The four-mile 1.25 percent grade started immediately and climbed the bluff on a shelf alongside a massive retaining wall. In addition to the Milwaukee, the Rock Island and Soo Line exercised trackage rights.

ABOVE ■ The camera is looking west from Chestnut Street at the junction between the 1869-vintage Minnesota Valley Railroad (at left) and the 1880 Short Line, which attacks the 1.25 percent grade at right. The Milwaukee and North Western shared the valley line from SPUD to Cliff Junction, two miles away on the other side of the Mississippi.

ABOVE ■ Downtown St. Paul sits on a sheer sandstone bluff overlooking the Mississippi and the Milwaukee Road. This train, headed to the St. Paul Ford Plant (note the auto parts boxcar) approaches Chestnut Street, where the Short Line hill climb begins.

LEFT ■ The Rock Island's road freights were broken up at Inver Grove Yard into transfers that took three or four different routes to yards in Minneapolis. One of them regularly traveled via the Milwaukee Road's Short Line. This one approaching Chestnut Street is returning to Inver Grove.

RIGHT ■ Remember open sided auto racks? These are descending the Short Line, returning from the auto transfer facility at South Minneapolis Yard. Joe is standing in St. Paul's Linwood Park. The high bluff in the distance marks the south bank of the Mississippi.

BELOW ■ A time freight, probably headed to the Pacific coast, climbs the Short Line as it approaches the parallel and aptly named Short Line Road, since renamed Ayd Mill Road. The transcontinental mainline has been severed in Minneapolis and abandoned completely from Montana west. This line has been single tracked and sees only a couple of transfer freights daily, plus the Amtrak EMPIRE BUILDER. The 50 mile per hour speed limit has been reduced to 40.

Left ■ Having just topped the grade out of Minneapolis, an eastbound transfer from South Minneapolis Yard to St. Paul's Pig's Eye Yard drifts down the Short Line hill under Selby Avenue.

Below ■ A Milwaukee F-unit has stubbed its toe negotiating the frozen mud of the wye next to the Minnesota Transfer roundhouse. The crew has applied elemental physics and persuasion to set things right.

Below ■ A transfer from the South Minneapolis Yard to St. Paul's Pig's Eye Yard crosses Cleveland Avenue in the St. Paul Midway. The units are working hard up the grade from the Mississippi River. The summit is about half a mile ahead. At the time there was an auto distribution facility at South Minneapolis, hence the empty auto rack. The signal marks Merriam Park, a 19th century commuter train stop, where the Minnesota Transfer enters from the left.

RIGHT ■ A pair of the prehistoric looking Baldwins cross the Short Line bridge over the Mississippi gorge that separates Minneapolis from St. Paul.

BELOW ■ Nearing the end of its journey, the overnight PIONEER LIMITED from Chicago curves to the Short Line bridge across the Mississippi that separates St. Paul from Minneapolis. The crossover is part of the junction with the East Side spur to the southeast Minneapolis grain elevator district.

South Minneapolis Engine Terminal

The Milwaukee's 8th Street coach yard was located a mile south of the Minneapolis depot. In earlier years the motive power was kept several blocks further south at the South Minneapolis roundhouse. When the roundhouse was torn down, the motive power moved up to share the coach yard, and a single track engine house was built. The coach yard site is now the Hiawatha light rail yard and shop.

LEFT & BELOW ■ The small engine terminal at the coach yard serviced three distinct groups of motive power. An all-Baldwin switcher fleet worked the Milwaukee Depot area, the grain elevators and mills stretching out Hiawatha Avenue toward Minnehaha Park, and the Pacific main line to the industrial suburb of Hopkins. They hauled everything back to the South Minneapolis Yard, where they assembled transfers for St. Paul's Pig's Eye Yard, where the road freights originated. In these studies, the idling switchers wait for the new day.

ABOVE & LEFT ■ The other denizens of the little engine terminal included the Es and FPs, painted Union Pacific Armour Yellow, that worked the passenger trains. Through the mid-1960s, five pairs of daily trains terminated in Minneapolis, four of them lasting into 1970. The orange Fs handled the transfers to Pigs Eye via the Short Line.

ALL ■ Daylight revealed a less dramatic, but no less interesting scene. This is actually a pretty new servicing facility, dating from the 1960s. Rather than install underground tanks, locos were fueled from tank cars. During one mid-winter break from college, the author found temporary work shoveling out the switches in this yard in the company of several winos and other street people. It was the best paying temp job I ever had.

Milwaukee Depot - Minneapolis

The Milwaukee Road's predecessor Minnesota Central built its first wood depot next to the west side milling district in 1864. It was replaced by a more substantial structure nearby along Washington Avenue. This in turn was replaced by the present Milwaukee Road depot in 1898. Although the railroads are gone, the depot and its fine five-track iron and wood train shed survive as a hotel.

The stub-ended depot had no runaround tracks. Everything that entered it had to back in or back out. All Rock Island and most Milwaukee Road trains terminated here and reversed directions to reach their coach yards. For Milwaukee Road's trains to the Pacific Coast, stopping in Minneapolis required a six-mile detour off its line across south Minneapolis, and half the detour was made backing up. Soo Line trains to and from the west (Winnipeg and Portal, ND) terminated in St. Paul, requiring a short backup move to pass through the Minneapolis depot. Those to and from the east (Duluth, Chicago and Sault Ste. Marie) terminated in Minneapolis and deadheaded to Shoreham Yard in northeast Minneapolis to be serviced. Joe barely caught the end of Rock Island's service, and missed the last Soo WINNIPEGER in 1967.

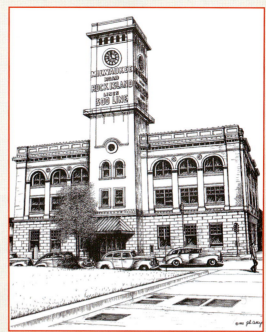

John Cartwright drawing

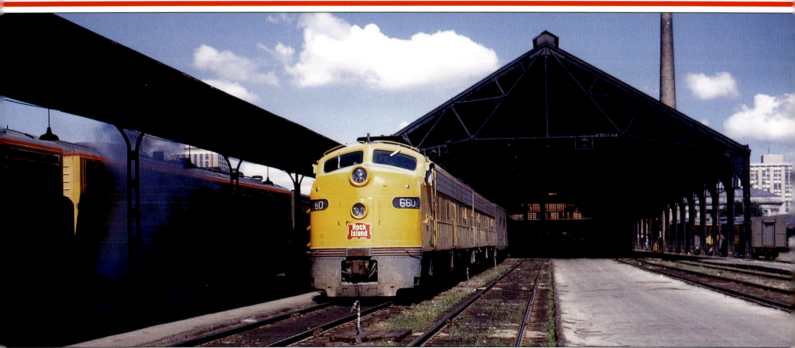

ABOVE ■ In its final few years of passenger service, the Rock Island's TWIN STAR ROCKET was downgraded to the Minneapolis-Kansas City PLAINSMAN. A few ex-Union Pacific E units were purchased to replace the E3s and other old power such as EMD BL2s.

BELOW ■ A Sperry Rail Service track detection car ties up along the back of the Milwaukee Depot.

ABOVE ■ The PIONEER LIMITED's power, its nocturnal duties over, traverses the depot's throat and crosses the viaduct over Washington Avenue on its way to the South Minneapolis engine terminal. Along with its overnight competitor, the CB&Q's BLACK HAWK, it made its last overnight run to Chicago in 1970.

LEFT ■ Among the Baldwin switchers that populated South Minneapolis, number 927 was different. Actually a road switcher carbody on switcher trucks, its short hood contained a steam generator for passenger train work. Here it's retrieving the PIONEER LIMITED's consist to the coach yard.

ALL ■ For much of the year, the AFTERNOON HIAWATHA's 8:20 PM arrival brought it under the Minneapolis train shed in darkness. Its worn diesels eased within a few feet of the bumper post, placing their rooftop exhausts under smoke jacks installed long ago for steam locomotives. The passengers carried their bags past the Post Office truck unloading mail, past the idling power, through the glass-enclosed concourse and into the high-ceilinged waiting room, its Victorian interior "modernized" when the streamliners appeared in the 1930s. A year after Joe captured these studies, the depot would see its last train.

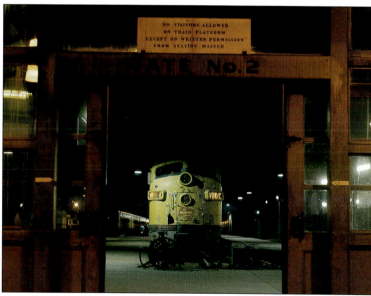

LEFT ■ FP9 #103A heads the MORNING HIAWATHA, preparing to depart Minneapolis. Under construction in the distance is the new Federal Reserve Bank Building. Its innovative suspension architecture was not successful and the feds have since replaced it – on the site of the Great Northern depot a few blocks away.

ABOVE ■ Plugged into the depot's steam line, a Milwaukee Road office car awaits the brass' return.

BELOW ■ The Soo Line used the Minneapolis Eastern to access the West Side milling district. The Alco DL640 "Dolly Sisters" were regular power on this run, which terminated at the Minneapolis & St. Louis Railway Transfer Yard, shown here.

BELOW ■ Next door to the Milwaukee Depot was the Minneapolis West Side milling district, two parallel rows of flour mills jammed side-by-side along the 1st Street water power canal. Railroads on multiple trestles accessed the complex. In addition, Minneapolis & St. Louis subsidiary Minneapolis Eastern ran down 2nd Street, the west edge of the mills and also the east edge of the Milwaukee Depot's two freight houses. The M&StL employed numerous Alco RS1s all over its system, and they were regular power in the milling district. This one has been repainted in C&NW colors, but is still lettered M&StL. The Milwaukee Road also had a small freight yard just south of its depot, the reason for this typical home-built bay window caboose.

Milwaukee Road to Hopkins

ABOVE ■ From 1913 to 1916, the Milwaukee Road dug a trench to grade separate its main line across south Minneapolis. Known as the 29th Street Depression, it replaced 39 grade crossings with bridges. To accommodate higher modern freight cars, the Milwaukee lowered the south track in the 1960s. Now abandoned, this right of way has been purchased by Hennepin County. A bike trail now occupies the north half, at left in this photo. The south half has been reserved for future rail transit.

LEFT ■ Grain empties head west, passing the suburban St. Louis Park depot. This weedy right of way is the Milwaukee's main line to the Pacific, an indicator of the carrier's poor health. The depot has been preserved in a nearby park. The line still extends to Montana, although it is now divided between two carriers. This end, now operated by regional Twin Cities & Western, serves only shippers within Minnesota.

Right ■ The Milwaukee shops rebuilt a group of geeps, chopping their noses and upgrading the horsepower to 2000. They emerged with GP20 plates on them. Two head a grain extra through St. Louis Park.

Above ■ Turning 180 degrees, an eastbound Milwaukee time freight is assaulting the rise leading to the St. Louis Park depot. There are actually three railroads in this photo. Visible at right is the parallel former Minneapolis & St. Louis, built through here in 1871. The Milwaukee appeared in 1882. Its purpose was to fix the Hastings & Dakota, which during 1869-1879 chose to bypass the Twin Cities on its way to western Minnesota. Once this new cutoff was in place, the western portion of the H&D was incorporated into the Pacific Extension. The bridge belongs to latecomer Minneapolis, Northfield & Southern. It appeared in 1915.

Left ■ Hopkins was a stand-alone small town about eight miles west of Minneapolis that became a suburb with a large concentration of industry. This is where the parallel Milwaukee Road and Minneapolis & St. Louis parted ways. That's the M&StL diverging to the right. The two railroads' depots still stand, on opposite sides of the tracks a couple of blocks apart. One of the ubiquitous Baldwin switchers works a spur track in the distance.

SPUD to Westminster Junction and Trout Brook Junction

The very first railroad in Minnesota, the St. Paul & Pacific, started at the St. Paul waterfront and used the valley of Trout Brook to climb away from the Mississippi on a 1.5-1.65 percent grade. Over the years, Trout Brook was placed in a sewer and its valley grew into a major throat seven tracks wide, plus a few switch leads. The C&NW subsidiary Omaha Road used the easternmost track on the embankment, and the Northern Pacific added a pair of double track lines on each side. In the middle and extending from here to St. Anthony Tower, just short of the Minneapolis city limits, was the GN's completely grade separated, four-track mainline, two for freight and two for passenger. The passenger tracks were taller and better ballasted than the freight tracks and passenger train speeds were impressive—as high as 70 miles per hour.

At Westminster Junction, the GN turned west, the C&NW/Omaha turned east and the NP continued straight. The result was the most complex junction in the Twin Cities. Essentially, Westminster was a wye with three railroads tunneling under it. The GN and C&NW constituted the wye and Westminster Tower was located along its southwest leg. The NP's two lines tunneled under the wye and came together to form a double track main line just north of Westminster. The third tunnel was built in 1909 to the west of the others by the Soo Line to reach its St. Paul yard and freight house. Westminster also featured a wild interchange track that made a steep and sharp S-curve from the Soo Line north of its tunnel to the C&NW north leg of the wye.

RIGHT ■ A C&NW freight has come off the former Chicago Great Western mainline from Iowa and has entered the multi-track throat leading north to Westminster Junction from the St. Paul Union Depot. It has only been a couple years since the merger, and CGW red is still common.

LEFT ■ Brake shoes smoking, a set of NP F-units takes the east leg of the wye that bypasses SPUD and heads for Dayton's Bluff. This is the bottom of a five-mile grade that begins halfway between Minneapolis and St. Paul. The rear of the train is still on 1.65 percent, the steepest part of the grade. The track at right is the former NP line to Duluth, soon to be abandoned.

Southern Pacific power makes an appearance at the same location. As the sign says, this is 3rd Street, just east of SPUD. The bridges in the distance carry I-94. Note the Armstrong linkage at right.

Above ■ Here's the post-merger EMPIRE BUILDER coming and going (opposite top), viewed from the Lafayette Boulevard bridge just south of Westminster Junction. On a sparkling morning, the eastbound BUILDER coils downgrade past Westminster Tower. The ex-NP main surfaces at right. It would later be single-tracked to maximize overhead clearance. The right hand track atop the retaining wall belonged to the Chicago & North Western and once carried the TWIN CITIES "400" out of town. The BUILDER is riding the eastbound passenger main.

Left ■ New BN power teamed with a GN FP45 descends the Trout Brook valley throat from Westminster Junction on ex-NP rails, passing under 7th Street. The rear of the train can be seen emerging from the subway under Westminster Junction. Because of its gentler grade leaving St. Paul, the NP line was chosen by BN as the primary freight route and it has already received welded rail, while the adjacent GN remains jointed.

ABOVE ■ The going-away shot captures traffic levels that remain today. Actually, it's busier now. The GN switcher is on its way downhill from the Mississippi Street coach yard to SPUD to retrieve some passenger cars. The track from the westernmost NP tunnel under Westminster ramps up to meet the other tracks just beyond the switcher. The yard tracks at right formerly staged cars for the downtown freight houses, which are out of the photo at right. Note the GMC city bus on the 7th Street bridge.

ABOVE ■ Despite the ex-NP units, this is the EMPIRE BUILDER, combined with the MORNING ZEPHYR from Chicago. The three CB&Q-painted switchers at right are an operational holdover from the Q practice of triple-headed switchers on transfer runs between the CB&Q Dayton's Bluff Yard and Minneapolis.

LEFT ■ The WINNIPEG LIMITED, behind twin E7s and with UP sleepers on the rear, arrives in St. Paul after its overnight run. It will pull past the SPUD roundhouse, visible beyond the locomotives, and back into the depot. The Big Sky Blue car is a former Chicago & North Western "400" coach. The stainless steel car with the blue window band was purchased used from the Missouri-Kansas-Texas.

LEFT ■ While the NORTH COAST LIMITED was overnight between North Dakota and Minnesota, the MAINSTREETER was its daytime counterpart. This view shows the two NP freight lines on either side of the embankment. When this was taken, the line emerging from a tunnel at left saw only switch runs. Since then, both NP lines have been single tracked and serve as a separated two-track main line today.

ABOVE ■ In 1968 the NORTH COAST LIMITED heads downgrade in full NP splendor through Westminster Junction. It's passing under the Lafayette Boulevard bridge. The stainless steel car in mid-consist is a Slumbercoach, and the one ahead of the observation is a foreign sleeper.

LEFT ■ The westbound EMPIRE BUILDER climbs and curves through Westminster.

ABOVE ■ The DAKOTAN, which has just left St. Paul Union Depot, passes the NORTH COAST LIMITED under the Lafayette Boulevard bridge. Little remarked outside Minnesota, the Great Northern's regional trains from the Twin Cities to North Dakota and Duluth were little gems. They were fast, clean, featured modest food service, and were well patronized. GN, and later BN, ran a quality service until the onset of Amtrak.

ABOVE ■ Having two mainlines between Minneapolis and Fargo, the GN put a day train on each. The WESTERN STAR ran via Willmar and the DAKOTAN, shown here, ran via St. Cloud. It collected passengers at intermediate towns and transferred them to the STAR at Fargo for points west. The consist is larger than usual today, hence the addition of an FB unit. That bit of trestlework in the foreground was needed because the C&NW's track was slightly too wide for the embankment.

RIGHT ■ A westbound Rock Island transfer dives under Westminster Junction on Northern Pacific trackage. It's headed for the Soo Line's Shoreham Yard in Minneapolis via the NP to Trout Brook Junction, then trackage rights on the Soo via the St. Paul branch to Cardigan Junction and then the main line to Shoreham.

LEFT ■ Viewed from the Chicago & North Western's north leg of the Westminster Junction wye, a BN freight behind a CB&Q SD24 climbs past the NP Mississippi Street roundhouse (out of the photo at right). The two sets of tracks that burrow under Westminster come together just ahead. Both are now single tracked to increase clearances. The ramped track at left, now consigned to maintenance of way equipment, was formerly an interchange with the Great Northern and C&NW. It crossed on a short bridge over the adjacent Soo Line's cut just north of its tunnel.

BELOW ■ The Soo Line's Roseport job to the Pine Bend oil refinery is descending the Northern Pacific's line where it splits into the two pairs of tracks that tunnel under Westminster Junction, visible in the distance. At left is the NP Mississippi Street roundhouse, soon to disappear. The partially plowed spur at right was formerly an interchange track to the C&NW and GN just west of Westminster.

ABOVE & RIGHT ■ Ex-NP geeps idle in front of the former Northern Pacific Mississippi Street roundhouse just north of Westminster Junction. This was the St. Paul terminal for NP power, located a short distance south of the company's Mississippi Street Yard, where its St. Paul freights tied up. In earlier years, the Minneapolis & St. Louis had trackage rights over the NP to St. Paul, and serviced its motive power at Mississippi Street. Redundant due to the BN merger, Mississippi Street was demolished a few years later.

ABOVE ■ An eastbound Rock Island transfer to Inver Grove Yard passes the Trout Brook Junction wye about a mile north of Westminster, where the Soo Line (Wisconsin Central) to Chicago diverged from the Northern Pacific two miles north of downtown St. Paul.

BELOW ■ NP U-boats meet at Trout Brook Junction. Oncoming U-25C #5616 was part of the first order of second generation, high-horsepower diesels on the Northern Pacific. It is leading an empty unit coal train to Montana. The Soo Line (Wisconsin Central) diverging at left hosted the LAKER to Chicago. It is now a bike trail.

Great Northern Mainline to Minneapolis

ABOVE & RIGHT ■ The former Great Northern Mississippi Street coach yard and shop was located next to the railroad's Jackson Street roundhouse, which maintained the passenger power and has been preserved and restored by the Minnesota Transportation Museum. The building and yard were on the same 1.5 percent grade as the mainline. Note the stepped-down roof sections.

ABOVE ■ Cleaners wash passenger cars at the former Great Northern Mississippi Street coach yard. All the former GN passenger trains were serviced here. The ex-NP trains used the NP coach yard near the St. Paul Union Depot. The CB&Q had a small locomotive and coach yard near the Great Northern depot in Minneapolis. All three facilities lasted until Amtrak.

ABOVE ■ During its last couple of years, the MAINSTREETER lost its head end business and continued as a small, full-service train that ran from St. Paul to the west coast. Here is passes the GN Mississippi Street coach yard and the Jackson Street roundhouse.

BELOW ■ A Rock Island transfer from the Minnesota Transfer yard to the RI Inver Grove Yard passes under Lexington Avenue in the St. Paul Midway. The tall stack belongs to Koppers Coke.

LEFT ■ One of the Minnesota Transfer's old Alco switchers was sold to Koppers Coke, located along the GN intercity main between Snelling and Lexington Avenues. There it shuffled cars around the coke plant. The last two active steam engines in the Twin Cities, former Soo Line 0-6-0s #346 and 353, lasted at Koppers until 1963. Both have been preserved and #353 is steamed annually by the Western Minnesota Steam Threshers Association at Rollag, MN.

BELOW ■ The sun sets over the GN four-track main line looking west from the Hamline Avenue footbridge toward Snelling Avenue. This transfer trails a Northern Pacific short wood caboose, repainted in BN colors. Freight cars in the Koppers Coke yard are barely visible at right.

BELOW ■ About to pass under Snelling Avenue, the GN GOPHER to Duluth overtakes a North Western freight that will terminate at East Minneapolis yard. The four-track main, with its higher speed passenger tracks at left, can be easily seen. The Koppers Coke plant is at left. Note the summit of the .5 percent grade between the two downtowns.

St. Anthony Tower

St. Anthony Tower was located in the St. Paul Midway district, just east of the Minneapolis city limits. Named for the adjacent St. Anthony Park neighborhood, it guarded the crossing of the Great Northern and the Minnesota Transfer. Complicating this track layout, the GN's double-tracked freight line from St. Paul crossed over the passenger main to enter Union Yard and the C&NW's adjacent East Minneapolis Yard. The Northern Pacific's "A Line" to the southeast milling district and downtown Minneapolis passed overhead on a substantial through truss bridge. Because of all the trackage rights, everything except the Soo Line and Milwaukee Road could show up at St. Anthony. Today the tower is gone and the junction is simplified somewhat, but all the basic routings remain. The NP "A" Line is now the University of Minnesota's Intercampus Busway.

ABOVE ■ The westbound MORNING ZEPHYR passes under Raymond Avenue. The Minnesota Transfer's yard is at right, and the Koppers Coke smokestack rises in the distance.

BELOW ■ Looking west from Raymond Avenue, a C&NW freight from Chicago crosses the GN passenger main to reach the East Minneapolis Yard.

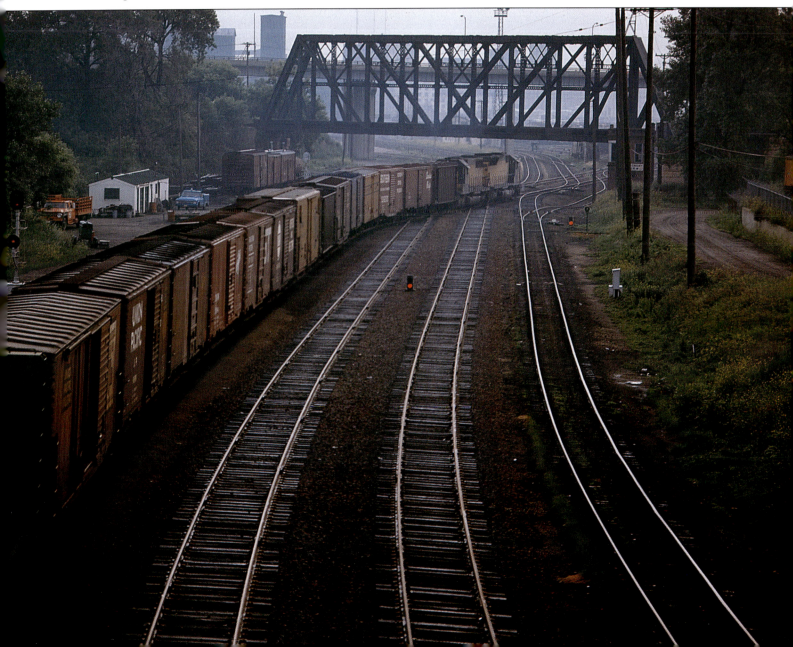

ABOVE ■ The all-rail iron ore train from the Missabe Range in northern Minnesota to the steel mill in Granite City, IL, passes St. Anthony Tower. Note the obsolete tell-tales hanging on both sides of the Northern Pacific bridge, since riding the tops had been outlawed for some time.

RIGHT ■ The AFTERNOON ZEPHYR shrank in its later years and lost its observation car, but was still a good looking train, seen here at St. Anthony Tower. The Northern Pacific "A" Line truss bridge crosses over it. The track at left is the interchange between the NP and the Minnesota Transfer.

ABOVE ■ Ex-Great Northern #406 was part of the first-ever SD45 order in 1966. It is entering Union Yard. Class engine #400 has been preserved by the Great Northern Historical Society and is stored at the Minnesota Transportation Museum's Jackson Street Roundhouse.

BELOW ■ A BN freight departs the east end of the former GN Union Yard, crossing the Minnesota Transfer and the GN passenger mainline at St. Anthony Tower. Sloping to the west, Union Yard used riding brakemen who rode into the bowl and hand-braked their cars to a halt. The yard has been replaced by an intermodal terminal.

RIGHT ■ Looking each way, the same train is led by a Burlington GP30 and an Erie-Lackawanna SDP45. Waiting for them to clear the junction is a C&NW freight headed into the East Minneapolis Yard behind a set of former Chicago Great Western F-units.

LEFT ■ An ex-CGW freight enters the GN's four-track main line to St. Paul. The nearest two tracks are for freight. The further pair, noticeably higher and better ballasted, are passenger-only. The track at far left leads to the Minnesota Transfer yards. The Transfer's freight to New Brighton also crossed the GN here.

BELOW ■ After it was absorbed into the C&NW, the Chicago Great Western road freights to Minneapolis were relocated from the Northern Pacific "A" Line and southeast Minneapolis yard to the North Western's nearby East Minneapolis Yard, accessed via the Great Northern. Strings of red F-units still led the trains, shown here exiting East Minneapolis and about to pass under the "A" Line.

ABOVE ■ A North Western caboose hop with CGW power enters St. Anthony Tower's interlocking, with the Raymond Avenue bridge in the distance.

RIGHT ■ Westbound ex-CGW F's pass under Raymond Avenue and prepare to cross the GN passenger main to enter the East Minneapolis Yard. The blue truck at right is sitting on the site of the St. Anthony Park depot. Until the 1890s, it was a stop on the Great Northern's hourly Minneapolis-St. Paul commuter trains. Passengers could transfer here to Minnesota Transfer trains to New Brighton. Amazingly, the depot survives as a house a block away.

BELOW ■ With an ex-CGW SD40 trailing, a C&NW road freight from Chicago waits at St. Anthony Tower. At right is the Minnesota Transfer's yard. The track diverging just beyond the tank cars at left is a seldom used connector between the parallel Great Northern and Northern Pacific main lines.

Above ■ Besides serving its Class One owners as a terminal road, the Minnesota Transfer possessed a 12-mile main line that ran north from St. Anthony Tower to New Brighton and Fridley. At one time it extended to Belt Line Junction where it met the combined NP-GN mainline to St. Cloud. After that connection was broken, it continued to serve a large number of on-line industries in the northern suburbs. This is one of the olive green SW1500s that replaced an earlier fleet of Alco switchers. The railroad is now owned by local short line Minnesota Commercial, which once again employs Alcos.

Above ■ The Northern Pacific's mainline between the cities divided at St. Anthony Park Junction, a short distance north of St. Anthony Tower. Diverging to the left is the Northern Pacific "A" Line to downtown Minneapolis via the southeast Minneapolis grain elevator district. This Rock Island transfer to Inver Grove is on the NP "B" Line that bypasses downtown and cuts a diagonal across northeast Minneapolis to Northtown Yard.

Below ■ An ex-CGW cow and calf set works the East Minneapolis Yard. There was a forest of grain elevators in southeast Minneapolis near the University of Minnesota and some of those rise in the distance.

LEFT ■ Exercising trackage rights that date back to the Minneapolis & St. Louis, a Chicago & North Western geep passes the NP's 18th Avenue SE tower. The tower for the adjacent GN Union Yard is at left, along with a line of idling switch engines.

RIGHT ■ To serve the southeast Minneapolis grain elevator complex, the GN mainline, the NP "A" Line, and Milwaukee Road East Side Spur converged at the 18th Ave. SE tower. Before being purchased by Chicago & North Western, the Chicago Great Western terminated at a small yard just beyond the tower. The Minneapolis & St. Louis passed through on its way to St. Paul via trackage rights over NP.

ABOVE ■ The short-lived Amtrak NORTH COAST HIAWATHA (Chicago-Seattle via the Milwaukee Road and the old NP) heads toward St. Paul through the grain elevator district of southeast Minneapolis near the University of Minnesota. In early Amtrak fashion, it's a mongrel consist with Milwaukee E-units up front and an ex-EMPIRE BUILDER Mountain-series obs on the rear.

Dinkytown

Joe was attending the University of Minnesota when most of these slides were taken. He lived on the edge of Dinkytown, the oddly named business district that serves the campus. On its way between the downtowns, the GN passenger main line passed through Dinkytown in a trench crossed by four closely spaced bridges that made good photo platforms. Trains roared through at about 50 miles per hour, the eastbound ones still accelerating away from the Stone Arch Bridge, so the lure for a photographer was irresistible.

LEFT ■ The MAINSTREETER trails a heavyweight business car as it passes under 15th Avenue SE. The 17th Avenue suspension footbridge is just beyond the signal bridge.

BELOW ■ The merger was starting to break down the Twin Cities motive power divide between GN and NP F-units and CB&Q E-units. The WESTERN STAR has an FB sandwiched between the Es. The intersection of 15th Avenue and 4th Street was elevated over the tracks and until 1954 was a streetcar junction served by the Como-Harriet, Oak-Harriet and Inter-Campus lines. The GN switcher is working the industrial lead alongside the passenger main. It led to the Pillsbury "A" Mill, the largest flour mill in Minneapolis and the last to survive, lasting into the 1990s.

ABOVE ■ The WESTERN STAR of 1968 sweeps under the 17th Avenue pedestrian bridge, which connects the University of Minnesota's baseball fields at left with the rest of the campus. The NP 18th Avenue SE Tower is barely visible at right.

BELOW ■ In 1968 the MAINSTREETER still carried considerable head-end traffic. A year or so later, it shrank to a six-car consist. The camera is facing east from the 15th Avenue SE bridge. The two tracks at right are the Northern Pacific "A" Line, relocated from the center of the U of M campus to here in 1922.

LEFT ■ Boxcars in the distance catch the rising sun as the NORTH COAST passes Dinkytown. The pair of tracks at far right is the NP "A Line" to the Minneapolis West Side milling district. Prior to 1922, it ran in a cut directly through the University of Minnesota's campus. Campus expansion caused the line to be relocated to this new alignment next to the GN in the Dinkytown trench. The NP track is now gone and its bridge across the Mississippi is a bikeway.

RIGHT ■ In later years it appears that the engine change to Q E-units was sometimes happening in Minneapolis, rather than St. Paul. Looking west from the University Avenue overpass in Dinkytown toward downtown, two bridges are visible in the distance. The arch span is the 10th Avenue bridge. Barely visible just beyond it is the I-35W bridge that collapsed in 2007.

BELOW ■ Visually arresting, this shot now is newsworthy. Joe is standing directly under the I-35W bridge that collapsed in 2007. The collapse crushed grain hoppers where Joe was standing.

Stone Arch Bridge

James J. Hill's great triumph in stone offers classic views of trains entering or leaving Minneapolis. S-curving across an angry Mississippi just below St. Anthony Falls, with the riverside mills and downtown skyline in the background, it was hard to take a bad photo of the bridge. After the Great Northern depot closed, it was single-tracked. Occasional freight trains were diverted over the bridge for a few years, then the tracks were removed altogether. After a decade of abandonment, the bridge became the first local recipient of federal Transportation Enhancement funds, converting it to a pedestrian and bicycle way that ties together a revived riverfront.

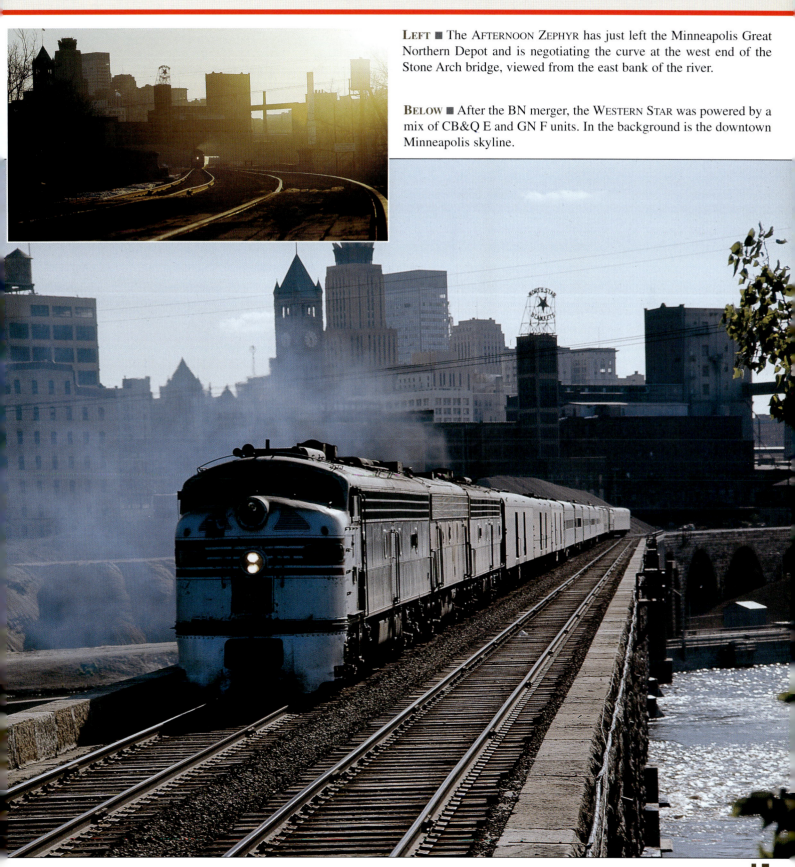

LEFT ■ The AFTERNOON ZEPHYR has just left the Minneapolis Great Northern Depot and is negotiating the curve at the west end of the Stone Arch bridge, viewed from the east bank of the river.

BELOW ■ After the BN merger, the WESTERN STAR was powered by a mix of CB&Q E and GN F units. In the background is the downtown Minneapolis skyline.

LEFT ■ A companion to the bottom photo shows the AFTERNOON ZEPHYR/EMPIRE BUILDER. Note that the first dome in the train is a silver ex-CB&Q. Condos, offices and a history museum now occupy most of the old mill buildings.

BELOW ■ Despite the NP power, this is the post-BN EMPIRE BUILDER, combined with the AFTERNOON ZEPHYR. The buildings closest to the river are the remains of the West Side milling district. Water-powered off a common canal under 1st Street, they gave Minneapolis its nickname "The Mill City". The mill district was penetrated by four different railroad trestles, now long gone. Freight cars were shifted and spotted on the trestles using car movers powered by water.

ABOVE ■ By 1971, BN had repainted some of its passenger equipment into the new green and white, but the EMPIRE BUILDER still sported mostly Big Sky Blue with a touch of Omaha Orange remaining. The four tall stacks in the distance belong to a power plant that was built by Twin City Rapid Transit to power its streetcar system. Much rebuilt, today it supplies steam to the University of Minnesota. The truss span that interrupts the bridge's stone arches was an unfortunate byproduct of extending river navigation north of St. Anthony Falls, a boondoggle that has been economically unsuccessful.

LEFT ■ Viewed from the downtown end of the Stone Arch Bridge, the truncated MORNING ZEPHYR of later years curves into downtown Minneapolis. Its rear car is crossing over the steel truss that was inserted to permit barge access to new locks that bypassed St. Anthony Falls. The bridge is now open to bicyclists and pedestrians.

ABOVE ■ For a brief period during the earliest days of Amtrak, Milwaukee Road E units could be seen crossing the Stone Arch Bridge.

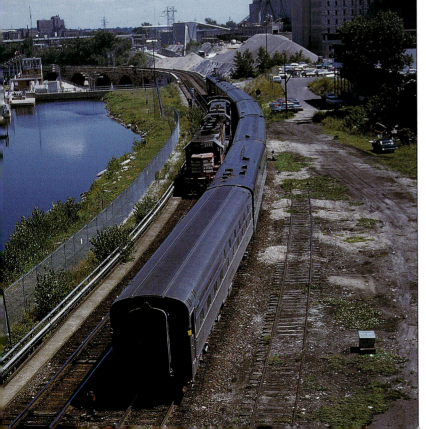

LEFT ■ Generally, the Stone Arch Bridge route was passenger only, with freights traveling via Minneapolis Junction. This caboose hop meeting the eastbound MAINSTREETER is an exception. The stub track at right used to lead to a long, three-tracked, high steel trestle that extended straight across the gravel piles in the distance to serve a row of riverfront mills.

Great Northern Depot

In 1900 Minneapolis had four downtown depots. One of them was called the Union Depot, but it hosted only a portion of the trains that entered the city. Some consolidation occurred in 1914, when the Great Northern Depot replaced the Union Depot at the foot of Hennepin Avenue next to the Mississippi River. The Minneapolis & St. Louis and the Chicago Great Western vacated their smaller nearby depots and moved into the Great Northern Depot, which also hosted the NP, CB&Q and C&NW. The C&NW's last "400" ran in 1963 and the CGW's overnight to Omaha came off in 1966, before Joe started taking pictures.

The GN Depot featured nothing but through tracks. Those trains that didn't terminate could travel east, north or west. The very sharp curve to the east was used by GN trains headed to Duluth or to St. Cloud via the east side of the Mississippi. The curve to the west was used by GN trains to Willmar or St. Cloud via the west side of the Mississippi, and by the M&StL. NP trains turned west, crossed the GN and immediately north under 4th Avenue North, dubbed "hole in the wall".

Even the numerous trains that terminated benefited. In most cases, their power and consists didn't have to change direction to reach their respective yards. The CB&Q yard was directly north of the depot across the east-west GN freight tracks. The C&NW crossed the same tracks to reach its yard and roundhouse a couple of miles up the river. The CGW took a hard right, crossed the river and Nicolle Island, and then backed into Boom Island Yard.

The GN Depot survived to host Amtrak for a few years. During that period, it was the only place in the Twin Cities to board a train, since the St. Paul Union Depot and the Minneapolis Milwaukee Road Depot had been abandoned. As a result, all the switching and consolidating of trains moved to the Great Northern Depot, which had seen little of that activity in the past.

Amtrak tried various combinations of trains. The EMPIRE BUILDER was the constant, although it sometimes used its traditional GN route via Willmar, MN, and eventually shifted to the former Northern Pacific between Minneapolis and Fargo. Amtrak also tried something called the NORTH COAST HIAWATHA. It combined the former NP NORTH COAST LIMITED route west of Minneapolis with the Milwaukee Road HIAWATHA route to Chicago. Sometimes it was combined with the EMPIRE BUILDER and sometimes it ran separately. It didn't last long.

Too big and expensive for the couple of daily trains that survived the Great Northern Depot was vacated and replaced by the new Midway station. After sitting empty for awhile, it was demolished and replaced by a new Federal Reserve Bank building. The tracks were removed in all directions except the GN's original east-west main line that crossed the Mississippi just to the north.

John Cartwright drawing

RIGHT ■ M&StL freight and Soo Line freight and passenger trains slipped between the west edge of the Great Northern depot and east side of the Minneapolis downtown post office via the double track Minneapolis Eastern that burrowed under Hennepin Avenue. RS1s were normal power for the switch runs connecting the old M&StL Cedar Lake Yard with the West Side milling district and its Railway Transfer Yard.

Above ■ A few hundred yards to the south sees a C&NW switcher-slug team turning the corner under the 3rd Avenue bridge. That's the Minneapolis main post office at right. A loading spur passed behind the row of pillars.

Below ■ Amtrak consolidated all Twin City passenger trains at the Great Northern depot. For a short time, the Milwaukee Road E-units crossed the Stone Arch bridge. In the background, a C&NW switcher/slug set follows the Minneapolis Eastern track that bypassed the GN Depot to reach the West Side milling district.

Above ■ A baggage handler at the Minneapolis Great Northern Depot.

Below ■ Dirty but still aristocratic, a Burlington E9 has arrived at Minneapolis with the Morning Zephyr.

Above ■ The Mainstreeter left Minneapolis for the west coast at 8:10 AM. The Burlington E-units at right probably just came off the overnight Chicago-Minneapolis Black Hawk, have turned on the wye and are about to back down to the coach yard.

BELOW ■ Mail is off-loaded from the westbound MORNING ZEPHYR in Minneapolis.

ABOVE ■ In an attempt at modernization, the colonaded Hennepin Avenue street entrance to the GN depot received this new sign in the mid-1960s. It was soon made obsolete by the BN merger. The last trains of the Chicago Great Western left the depot in 1966, the C&NW's "400" disappeared in 1963 and the Minneapolis & St. Louis' last doodlebug quit in 1960.

ABOVE ■ Following the BN merger, the route of the former GN WESTERN STAR was changed to use the Northern Pacific's passenger route from the Minneapolis depot to Northtown Yard. The former route had the WESTERN STAR make a sharp right turn out of the depot. That had the effect of shortening the platform for the long train, perhaps requiring a double stop. Following the NP route through the "hole in the wall" probably added a couple of car lengths to the platform. It also used a more lightly traveled line, reducing possible congestion delays near Minneapolis Junction on the old route. Note that the first blue coach is an ex-C&NW car.

ABOVE ■ The EMPIRE BUILDER'S Great Dome lounge attendant awaits the departure from Minneapolis. Note the diner at right.

ABOVE ■ A car knocker fills the EMPIRE BUILDER'S water tanks after its arrival in Minneapolis from Chicago.

ABOVE ■ Sack mail is unloaded from the combine of the MORNING ZEPHYR, just in from Chicago.

Left ■ When Joe learned that the Empire Builder was within days of losing its Railway Post Office, he captured this Railway Mail Service clerk at Minneapolis with the tools of his trade.

Right ■ Mail is unloaded in Minneapolis from the eastbound afternoon Gopher, just in from Duluth. Note that the RPO car is lettered for the Empire Builder.

During the early Amtrak days, some unusual observation cars found their way onto the short-lived North Coast Hiawatha. This appears to be a former California Zephyr dome-observation.

ABOVE ■ The former EMPIRE BUILDER observation *Appekunny Mountain* is being wyed before leaving town on the NORTH COAST HIAWATHA. Note the BN office car on the next track.

RIGHT ■ An early Amtrak NORTH COAST HIAWATHA trails what appears to be a Seaboard Air Line SILVER METEOR observation.

LEFT ■ The presence of a "foreign" observation car dates this view as the post-Amtrak EMPIRE BUILDER or NORTH COAST HIAWATHA. Also, note the "Mountain" series ex-EMPIRE BUILDER observation car on the adjacent track. This view looks out the east end of the depot, where a BN SW1500 is ready to switch consists.

BELOW ■ Four E-units on the front end imply that this is the combined EMPIRE BUILDER/NORTH COAST HIAWATHA from Chicago, about to be divided into two trains between Minneapolis and the west coast.

ABOVE ■ The headlight of an approaching train backlights the station employees, waiting on the Track 7 platform to load their carts of mail and express.

BELOW ■ The St. Paul Union Depot and the Minneapolis Milwaukee Road Depot both closed when Amtrak took over the nation's passenger trains in 1971. All switching work and power changes moved to the Minneapolis Great Northern Depot. In its later years, the GN depot had not been known as a place where much switching occurred or detached locomotives or passenger cars sat, but that changed. Milwaukee Road E-units were a short term visitor during those early days of mix-and-match Amtrak consists.

Viewed from the south, the Great Northern Depot's Hennepin Avenue façade is visible above the train sheds. The Mississippi River is just out of the frame at right.

ABOVE ■ The Omaha freight house was located two blocks north of the Great Northern Depot. It still stands, converted to condominiums, on 4th Avenue North near the Mississippi River. All track has now disappeared from this neighborhood.

BELOW ■ A Minneapolis & St. Louis boxcar stands alongside the Omaha freight house.

The CB&Q power and passenger trains were serviced at a small engine terminal/coach yard on the riverfront just north of the Great Northern Depot. The MORNING ZEPHYR from Chicago has been backed into the shed for servicing during its 45 minute layover. Then it will depart Minneapolis as the AFTERNOON ZEPHYR.

ABOVE & RIGHT ■ When C&NW absorbed the M&StL and the CGW, it inherited CGW roundhouses on Boom Island and State Street in St. Paul, as well as the M&StL's large Cedar Lake shops. Its own former Omaha Road roundhouse in north Minneapolis was at the end of a couple miles of non-revenue trackage, so it was declared redundant and was abandoned in 1969. It was already out of service when Joe took these views.

Great Northern Willmar Line, Monticello Line

LEFT ■ The NORTH COAST LIMITED s-curves under 1st Street, across the GN Willmar line and into the GN depot. A former NORTH COAST LIMITED tail car, now privately owned and renamed *Twin Cities Club*, will be attached to the rear for the run to Chicago.

BELOW ■ Upon leaving the GN depot, the MAINSTREETER crossed the GN main and passed under 1st Street, curved sharply to the right and passed under 4th Avenue N., known as the "hole in the wall".

The EMPIRE BUILDER is about to pass under Highway 12, with the Kenwood water tower in the distance. The tracks at far left are the Minneapolis & St. Louis, now a bike trail. The other yard tracks are gone.

ABOVE ■ The first railroad to extend west from Minneapolis in 1867 was the St. Paul & Pacific, which skirted the north edge of downtown. It became the GN's Willmar Division, and was lined with yards, freight houses and industrial spurs. All except the two main tracks are now gone. In 2009, the area to the right will see a new commuter rail station, adjacent to a new Twins' baseball stadium. The Hiawatha LRT line is being extended to a new station located over the tracks on the 5th Street bridge, above the TOFC trailers.

ABOVE ■ Looking the other way through the "hole in the wall," the MAINSTREETER skirts the west edge of the NP Lower Yard, which filled the block between 1st and 2nd Streets. Two blocks north of the engine was a steam era roundhouse. Across the street to the left of the locomotives was the original Soo Line Minneapolis depot and freight house. All these tracks are now gone, replaced by condos.

Right ■ The EMPIRE BUILDER exits Minneapolis via the Willmar line. The cabooses in the distance sit at Lyndale Junction, where the Monticello line to St. Cloud diverges. The extremely long caboose is one of a kind, home-built for service on the Hutchinson branch, which leaves the main line at Wayzata, 13 miles west of Minneapolis.

Below ■ Viewed from the Plymouth Avenue overpass, a freight behind U25Bs follows the former GN Monticello line though Wirth Park on the west edge of Minneapolis. This line, which formerly offered an alternate route to St. Cloud west of the Mississippi River, was truncated at Monticello and today hosts a daily local to switch a handful of shippers near Osseo.

RIGHT ■ A GP9/F combination powers a southbound freight, also at Plymouth Avenue. The signal in the distance marks the approach to a junction with the line that barely be seen at top center beyond the telegraph poles. Originally the Electric Short Line Terminal, it provided a joint downtown Minneapolis entrance for the Electric Short Line, which became the Minnesota Western or "Luce Line", and the Minneapolis, Northfield & Southern. Both carriers aspired to be interurbans, but never strung wire. Today, Canadian Pacific owns the MN&S and still sends a switch run down a truncated Electric Short Line Terminal to service a couple of shippers. The Luce Line became part of the Minneapolis & St. Louis, then the C&NW, which in turn was swallowed by the Union Pacific. Several miles survive to reach industries west of Minneapolis, and a daily UP turn follows the GN to that junction just around the corner, then out the wobbly Luce Line to suburban Plymouth.

BELOW ■ Joe chased the freight headed by the Big Sky Blue geep. Here it is alongside US52, now County Road 81, which it parallels through the suburbs of Crystal, Brooklyn Park and Osseo. This line also saw passenger service into the 1960s. Today it is being considered a candidate for light rail transit.

LEFT ■ A northbound freight on the Monticello line leaves Hennepin County when it crosses this bridge over the Crow River. The Monty Local, as the present day turn is dubbed, seldom goes north of Osseo, which is 13 miles from Minneapolis. The track remains in place another 23 miles to Monticello, but the only traffic today is occasional shipments of nuclear waste from the power plant there.

Great Northern Depot to Coon Creek Junction

The GN and NP built side by side east of the Mississippi from Northtown Yard in Minneapolis to St. Cloud. It looked like a double track railroad and by mutual agreement it was operated as one. The GN's line to Duluth diverged at Coon Creek Junction.

ABOVE ■ The MORNING ZEPHYR from Chicago has backed onto the GN bridge over the Mississippi as part of wyeing it for the return trip. It will pull ahead, turn left into the GN depot and return to Chicago as the AFTERNOON ZEPHYR.

LEFT ■ Just east of the Mississippi, the GN grade-separated its right of way through the Old St. Anthony neighborhood of northeast Minneapolis. Freight trains used this route to bypass passenger congestion on the Stone Arch Bridge and through the Great Northern depot. However, these tracks served passenger trains headed for Duluth or for St. Cloud via the line along the east side of the Mississippi.

BELOW ■ Joe happened upon an unusual piece of GN work equipment parked at the Minneapolis Great Northern Depot powerhouse. The car was originally built in 1905 as #A-22, the business car of Louis Hill, then GN President and son of James J. Hill. The entire far end was a pair of large doors opening onto a large empty room, a rolling garage where Hill could carry his automobile along with him. Originally an all-wood car, it was rebuilt over the years, receiving a steel underframe and steel sheathing. Converted to work train service in 1950, it survived and joined the collection of the Mid-Continent Railway Museum in 1972.

RIGTH & BELOW ■ In 1901 the Wisconsin Central built a yard and roundhouse on Boom Island, located in the Mississippi River just north of downtown. It reached the east riverbank via a bridge to adjacent Nicollet Island and a second bridge to a connection with the GN on the east bank of the river. WC also built a freight house near the foot of Hennepin Avenue, across from the old Union Depot. These facilities were sold in 1909 to the Chicago Great Western. Over time, the east channel around Boom Island was filled in. The Boom Island Yard and roundhouse lasted until the C&NW takeover in 1968. For awhile thereafter, a switch run used a remnant of the yard, and this is it. The bridge remains in place today for bicycles and pedestrians to access Boom Island Park.

One of the NP's first SD45s, numbered for its horsepower, sits outside the old Northtown roundhouse. The roundhouse was replaced by the modern Northtown diesel shop a few blocks to the north. Today it handles all of BNSF's locomotive maintenance in the Twin Cities.

Two years later, the merger had happened and geeps were being mixed.

BELOW ■ Between Northtown Yard and St. Cloud, the GN and NP jointly operated their single track mains as a combined double track, so no transition was necessary following the 1970 BN merger. The line is straight, flat and fast. In 1968 a matched set of NP Fs still proclaims the "Main Street of the Northwest".

BELOW ■ The former joint NP/GN line through Coon Creek saw both the WESTERN STAR, here with a new SDP40, the GN GOPHER and BADGER to Duluth, and the NORTH COAST LIMITED and MAINSTREETER. Today, Amtrak's EMPIRE BUILDER still passes through, and efforts are underway to reinstate a Duluth train.

LEFT ■ In the mid-1960s, GN combined the FAST MAIL with the WESTERN STAR, its secondary Minneapolis-Seattle train. The result was this very long creature that trailed a rider-baggage car. The rear brakeman sat inside that single window ahead of the rear vestibule. The Minnesota Transportation Museum now owns one of these cars.

ABOVE ■ There must have been some sort of run-through arrangement with Erie-Lackawanna, but the BN crews can't be too happy with this old F2. It is stopped on the eastbound main waiting to get into Northtown. There's a handwritten note next to the MU cable cover, "This head rewired to match BN unit".

RIGHT ■ At Coon Creek Junction, the transcontinental mainline swings left and the ex-GN line to Duluth diverges to the right. The conductor of a Duluth-bound freight stands on the caboose steps, ready to snag his orders as his train and the operator prepares to retrieve the sticks.

LEFT ■ Looking north from Coon Creek Junction, the eastbound North Coast spirals into the curve behind an F in BN colors. In 2009, this line will see the startup of Northstar Corridor commuter trains.

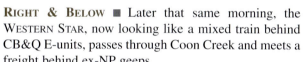

RIGHT & BELOW ■ Later that same morning, the WESTERN STAR, now looking like a mixed train behind CB&Q E-units, passes through Coon Creek and meets a freight behind ex-NP geeps.

Above ■ In later years the NORTH COAST lost its observation car, but the rest of the classy consist remained intact. This view looks south at Coon Creek. Note the semaphore signals in the distance.

Above ■ The afternoon GOPHER'S crew gets a wave from the Coon Creek operator as it's about to swing onto the Duluth line at left. The BADGER was the morning local in both directions. The GOPHER was the afternoon express both ways. The author remembers riding this train and timing mileposts at 90 miles per hour on the arrow straight track north of here.

Right ■ Dirty Fs in Big Sky Blue pass through Coon Creek.

ABOVE ■ Coal empties for Montana head west through Coon Creek. The second locomotive is an ex-NP U25C.

Soo Line, West to East

Soo Line was freight-only by the time Joe began shooting. Its through freights stayed on the northern fringes of Minneapolis, calling at Shoreham Yard in northeast Minneapolis, and Humboldt Yard, three miles to the west across the Mississippi. Our photo coverage travels from west to east.

ABOVE ■ Humboldt Yard borders a residential neighborhood in north Minneapolis. Humboldt was built after Shoreham and was easier to switch. Shoreham was laid out on a sweeping curve and its east throat climbed a steep grade. Cars were dropped into the bowl by gravity and the yard engine often lost sight of them before they reached the standing cars. The eastbound grade sometimes required helpers to start a long freight. In contrast, Humboldt Yard was straight and flat.

BELOW ■ The Twin Cities saw more than its share of Fairbanks-Morse diesels. They powered the HIAWATHAS in the 1950s. Some lasted into the early 1970s on the rosters of the Milwaukee Road and Minneapolis, Northfield & Southern. The Soo Line used these boxy switchers at Shoreham and, shown here, at Humboldt Yard.

ABOVE ■ At Camden in north Minneapolis, a transfer from Humboldt Yard to Shoreham Yard approaches the bridge over the Mississippi River. The track at left follows the river's west bank to downtown Minneapolis, serving numerous industries on the way. Until at least the 1960s, Camden had a depot that was staffed with an operator.

LEFT ■ Going away, the same transfer crosses the Mississippi River on the Camden bridge, which featured a wye at its west end. The track at right leads to downtown Minneapolis.

Above ■ The Soo's modern power was all EMD, but it did try a few General Electric U30Cs. Teamed with a geep, one of them climbs the grade eastbound out of Shoreham Yard. The train is crossing Central Avenue. The switch in the distance is where the high line bypass around Shoreham diverges. Until 1953, the flat area at right was the interchange with the 1.5 mile electrified Minneapolis Filtration Plant Railway. It climbed a 5 percent grade alongside Reservoir Boulevard to serve the Filtration Plant.

Opposite Page, Inset ■ A mile west of Shoreham, the Soo Line crossed over the Northern Pacific's Northtown Yard. The NP roundhouse, since replaced by a new, large diesel house, is visible at far left. Two interchanges descended from this fill. The one on the north side reached the remnant of interurban Minneapolis, Anoka & Cuyuna Range. The other, on the south side of the tracks, connected with the NP. It was regularly used by the Minneapolis, Northfield & Southern, which had trackage rights through here to Shoreham. The MN&S was eventually purchased by the Soo, and both are now operated by Canadian Pacific.

Left ■ In suburban New Brighton, the Soo Line's main to Chicago crossed the Minnesota Transfer. Also known as Bulwer Junction, it saw freight interchange between the two roads and was staffed into the 1970s. The depot has been preserved and moved to a nearby county park.

ABOVE ■ A Soo Line freight approaches Cardigan Junction from the west. In the distance is the bridge over I-694 and directly beyond it the St. Paul branch diverges to the right.

Above ■ At Cardigan Junction, through freights set out cars for the Soo Line's St. Paul branch. The Soo built through here in 1887, and many of the original wood board and batten standard depots survived into the 1970s.

Left ■ One of the pair of Alco DL640s, locally known as "the Dolly sisters," rolls a caboose hop through the suburb of Little Canada on the St. Paul branch. This is probably a transfer returning to Shoreham Yard empty.

RIGHT ■ A westbound time freight soars over the St. Croix River on the Soo's spectacular high bridge north of Stillwater. It replaced an earlier low-level span that sat at the base of grades in both directions.

Minneapolis Northfield & Southern

The Minneapolis Northfield & Southern was Minneapolis' small home-grown success story. It started in 1910 as the Minneapolis, St. Paul & Dubuque Electric Traction Company, with every intention of building an interurban to Dubuque. Its rails never reached beyond Northfield, MN and it never strung wire. Instead, it became the first American railroad powered entirely by internal combustion, and its pioneer gas electric locomotive #100 survived to join the Minnesota Transportation Museum's collection.

Reorganized as the MN&S in 1918, it settled into a profitable new role as a Twin Cities freight bypass. From interchanges with the Rock Island and Milwaukee Road in Northfield, and the Great Western in Randolph, it bridged traffic to the Milwaukee Road, Great Northern, Northern Pacific and Soo Line, knocking days off the time of direct interchange through the congested cities. It also cultivated numerous on-line suburban shippers. The MN&S, better known as the "Dan Patch Line" (original owner Marion Savage owned the champion harness racing horse Dan Patch), was beloved for its clean, attractive equipment, undulating right of way and entrepreneurial spirit.

ABOVE ■ MN&S replaced its steam locomotives on road freights with big Baldwin center cab diesels. These were succeeded by EMD SW1200 and SW1500 switchers with Flexicoil trucks, often running in four-unit lashups. In 1968, MN&S bought some real road power, a pair of SD39s, including number 41, shown here at the Glenwood shop.

LEFT ■ In addition to its centercabs, the Dan Patch rostered a single Baldwin DRS615. Number 15, seen here inside the Glenwood Shop, was regularly assigned to the High Line, the company's original trackage through Bloomington and Richfield to the southern edge of Minneapolis.

BELOW ■ Trains of 50-75 cars followed three or four EMD switchers, as is the case here in the suburb of St. Louis Park.

ABOVE ■ A typical dark blue MN&S caboose (some were white) trails a freight through the western suburbs of Minneapolis.

RIGHT ■ Although better known for its Baldwins, MN&S owned a pair of Fairbanks-Morse switchers. Both survive today. Number 10 is on display in Chicago & North Western colors in Milton Junction, WI. Number 11 was sold to Hallett Dock in Duluth and is now in the collection of the Lake Superior Railroad Museum. They worked the Glenwood Yard.

Outstate

ABOVE & BELOW ■ Within Minnesota, the Milwaukee Road owned five branch lines that built west from the Mississippi via tributary rivers valleys. Intended more as steamboat feeders, they carried little traffic and none survive today. Most northerly of these was the Hastings & Dakota, which built up the Vermillion River and out onto the prairies of western Minnesota, completely bypassing the Twin Cities in the process. This was not a smart move. The eastern portion from Hastings to Farmington succumbed in 1935. A new mainline was built from Minneapolis to Cologne in 1882, and the remainder of the H&D between Farmington and Cologne eked out a living serving local shippers until 1979. One of these was the Crystal Sugar plant in Chaska. For feedstock, it relied on sugar beets that grew all along the line to South Dakota. These traveled seasonally in downgraded coal hoppers. Here empties slowly return west between Chaska and Cologne.

Hudson

The ruling grade on the C&NW's "400" route to Chicago was the westbound 1.35 percent climb from the St. Croix River at Hudson, WI. On the Minnesota side, there was a sharp curve at the base of the grade. Just before the curve was a swing bridge across the river that was sometimes opened for boats. The inability to run for the westbound grade made Hudson a helper station for many years.

ABOVE ■ A Chicago-bound freight crosses the C&NW St. Croix River bridge, viewed from the Minnesota side on a foggy day. Beyond the bridge is the Hudson, WI depot, built on a long causeway in the middle of the river. Just past the depot, the branch to Elllsworth, WI split off. A bit further, in North Hudson, were the car shops of the Omaha Road. They remain intact today, used for light industry and warehousing.

ABOVE ■ In fairer weather, this was the view looking west at track level. Lakeland Junction is not visible from here, but is located at the two CN boxcars at right. Until 1979, the C&NW crossed the Milwaukee Road's Stillwater branch, which ran up the west bank of the river. The North Western's own Stillwater branch diverged to the right at the same location. It ran right next to the Milwaukee Road, creating what looked like a double track railroad with wobbly light rail. The North Western's branch still runs north to Bayport, where it serves Andersen Windows and a power plant.

RIGHT ■ Dynamic brakes whine as a North Western freight descends the formerly double-tracked eastbound 1.35 percent grade to the St. Croix bridge. This was the ruling grade on the line and required helpers in the past.

LEFT & BELOW ■ Headed for Chicago, this train came from Superior, WI, via an indirect route, because of weight restrictions on the bridge at Chippewa Falls. It followed the old route of the NAMAKEGON motor train via New Richmond, turning east at the Northline wye.

ABOVE ■ C&NW needed some heavy haul power and picked up a group of Alco C628s from Norfolk & Western. They entered service before repainting, hence the spectacle of this brute quintet muscling iron ore eastbound along the "400" route at Northline, WI, a few miles east of Hudson.

LEFT ■ The "big I&M" was the daily time freight that connected Iowa and Minnesota. It traveled the Milwaukee's pioneer 1864 line that went straight south from the Twin Cities through Northfield and Austin to Iowa. It was the first through rail route to Chicago via Prairie du Chien and Madison, WI, eclipsed in 1872 by the River Division up the west bank of the Mississippi. The location is the Highway 3 overpass in suburban Eagan. No longer a through route, it survives today as an industrial spur run by short line Progressive Rail.

Hinkley Tower

BELOW ■ Hinckley Tower guarded the crossing of the Great Northern and Northern Pacific's competing Twin Cities-Duluth main lines. The NP line also hosted the Milwaukee Road on trackage rights. Joe photographed it while both lines were still in full operation. Deciding it didn't need both, BN shifted all operations to the GN and abandoned much of the NP. Today, the tower is gone. The NP yard remains intact north of the junction and the depot is now the Hinkley Fire Museum. South of the junction, the NP is intact as far as North Branch, operated by short line St. Croix Valley. Most of the remainder of the line is now a bike trail. A southbound Duluth-St. Paul freight on the former NP crosses the GN's Duluth-St. Paul line at the tower.

BELOW ■ The NP and the Milwaukee Road kept their power at the NP's roundhouse in Duluth, located on Garfield Avenue. The city is laid out on the side of a high ridge overlooking Lake Superior.

Left ■ Elsewhere in the tower, another desk retains its telegraph key, sounder and classic two-piece extendable telephone. Note the levers for the train order semaphore, mounted on the wall behind the telegraph sounder.

Right ■ Trains are no longer marked up using chalk, so a few nails have been pounded into the train board, making it suitable for posting important paper.

Left ■ The operator sits at her desk, equipped with dial telephone, company radio and a manual typewriter. As with all such places, important documents were hung on the wall.

Below ■ The Hinkley Tower train order semaphore.

Left ■ The tower lined routes with a classic an Armstrong interlocking plant.

Transition to Black and White

Beginning in 1970, Joe started shooting and printing black and white along with color slides. He began turning out elegant studies that presaged his lifelong interest in documenting industrial decline. We end the book with a sample of that early black and white work.

ABOVE, BOTH ■ The Soo Line's 1887-vintage wood depots were still staffed in 1970, but would not last long. Withrow, northeast of St. Paul, where the main lines to Chicago and Sault Ste. Marie divide, was a tiny place with a bar, a ballroom and a few houses.

ABOVE ■ A six-axle Alco tiptoes down the Chicago Great Western's doubtful iron on the Cannon Valley line from Cannon Falls to Red Wing.

ABOVE ■ Relegated to work train service, an old Pullman freezes and rusts next to the Chicago & North Western's Winona, MN depot in 1972.